TURQUOISE TREASURES

Ketoh made in the early 1900's, set with Tiffany (Cerrillos) turquoise. Choker is hand-made of wrought silver beads set with clusters of turquoise.

TURQUOISE TREASURES

The Splendor of Southwest Indian Art

Photography by Jerry Jacka
Text by Spencer Gill

ISBN: Casebound edition 0-912856-21-1; Paperbound edition 0-912856-25-4
Library of Congress Catalog Number 75-7141
Copyright© 1975 by Graphic Arts Center Publishing Co.
2000 N.W. Wilson • Portland, Oregon 97209 • 503/224-7777
Designer • Robert Reynolds
Printer • Graphic Arts Center
Bindery • Lincoln & Allen
Printed in the United States of America

Variety in this collection of Persian turquoise indicates the range of grades and colors which can come from one source. Identifying the origin of a particular piece of turquoise can often be difficult, even for experts.

High grade Morenci turquoise in various forms: center and center left, veins as they come from the mine; center right, semi-finished; right foreground, polished and ready for mounting; upper right, ketoh by Charles Loloma; lower left, necklace of disc beads and slabs of Morenci turquoise.

Zuni jewelry of the 1930's set with Morenci turquoise. Nugget is unusual seafoam Morenci and slabs are high grade Morenci turquoise.

Green, spider web Kingman turquoise stone weighs 3,100 carats. Sandcast necklace is Navajo.

Turquoise is a gem with a rare quality. None other can match it for the countless centuries it has been treasured in legend and history, from the ornaments of the ancient Egyptians and early Persians to the jewelry of present-day Indians of the American Southwest.

Tiny scarabs—little beetles symbolic of good fortune—shaped by the jewelsmiths of the earliest Pharaohs find their counterpart in the fetishes of birds, frogs and snakes of the prehistoric Indians and in the figurines carved by the Zuni craftsmen of today. The turquoise-adorned bridles of distant Tibetans meant safe journey for horse and rider and today's horseowners who can display the silver and turquoise of Navajo silversmiths consider themselves especially fortunate.

Although the ancient mines of the Sinai are little worked today, the mines of Persia and the American Southwest continue to produce quality turquoise as they have for centuries. And at no time in history has the popularity of turquoise been so great as it is today; in particular, for the jewelry created by the Indian artists and craftsmen (and craftswomen) of the pueblos and hogans.

In these pages, some of the history of turquoise is presented, some facts, some legends, and especially, photographs of turquoise treasures of the Indians of the American Southwest.

Bluebird wore a beautiful robe of blue beads and on his head a bright blue cloud. In his right hand he held a rattle made of blue turquoise and in his left a stalk of blue corn. And when the people asked what he had brought, Bluebird said: I bring you blue sky, summer rain and soft corn. From a Navajo myth

Turquoise is a legendary jewel for the Indians of the American Southwest, sharing in the power of the creative spirit which animates all things in nature. It comes from the earth, and in its color there is the blue of the sky, the pale blue of early morning, the bright blue of mid-day, the electric blue that darkens with the approaching thunder clouds, and the varied blues of the great ocean.

All things in the world, including people, were formed in the womb of the earth and brought up into daylight. And from the earth came the many spirits and forces of nature.

The Hopi speak of a gentle spirit, Hard Beings Woman or Woman of Hard Substances, mother of the universe who is associated with turquoise and shell. She is of the earth, but is also of the heavens where the moon and the stars are hers. She created a youth, the earth-spirit of crops, and a maiden, Childbirth Water Woman, the spirit protecting human fertility. The sun spirit, ornamented with eagle feathers, shell beads and turquoise, crosses the sky each day and completes his journey at the home of Hard Beings Woman in the western ocean.

There are many Navajo myths of the birth of the Turquoise Goddess or Changing Woman. She was born on a mountain top as a small turquoise image after Mother Earth and Father Sky had come together. She grows in beauty from young to

Hathor, an early Egyptian sky goddess, was said to have been associated with both fertility and turquoise. She was represented as a wild cow of the marshes and stood so that her legs divided the earth into four parts. Her belly indicated the heavens. Horus, the sun god, symbolized as a falcon, flew each day from east to west, entered her mouth at evening and was reborn each dawn.

The scarab beetle was sacred to the Egyptians and was a treasured symbol of good luck. Tiny scarabs, no larger than a fly, and larger amulets were carved from turquoise.

The Egyptian word for beads was *sha-sha* and the syllable *sha* was the word for luck.

The Pharaohs considered the circle as a symbol of eternity and a ring as a sign that life has no beginning and no ending.

In Egypt and Persia, amulets carved of turquoise were buried on the chest, eyes and forehead of the dead.

In Persia it was said that if you looked upon a piece of turquoise when you first arose in the morning, you would have a day without trouble.

Good fortune was said to come to those who saw the reflection of the new moon on a copy of the Koran, on the face of a friend or on a turquoise stone.

Persian men wore turquoise rings to ensure safe journey whenever they travelled.

The Tibetans prized amber, coral and turquoise as symbols of good health and good fortune. If a turquoise became pale in color, it was a warning of danger and an indication that the stone had lost its power to protect. A stone which had failed its owner would be dyed a deeper shade and sold to strangers.

In remote valleys of Tibet turquoise was hung around the neck of a favorite pony to ward off evil and placed on bridles to prevent missteps or injury to the horse or rider.

Discorides, a Greek physician to the Romans, prescribed the wearing of coral to prevent skin ailments.

Mohammed-ibn-Mansur wrote in the 13th century: "whoever owns the true turquoise set in gold will not injure any of his limbs when he falls, whether he be riding or walking, so long as he has the stone with him." He also wrote that the eye is strengthened by looking at turquoise.

Arabian astrologers are said to have brought the idea of birthstones into Europe during the 15th century. The stone for December may be lapis lazuli or turquoise and for the sign of the Zodiac, Capricorn, garnet or turquoise.

old, changing as the seasons change, an ever-living spirit, maturing and become young again in a continuing cycle of life. In some stories, she has an island home in the western ocean where the sun-bearer comes at the end of day. In other versions, she has a twin sister, White Shell Woman, who makes her home in the ocean. From the ocean she sends the spring breezes and the summer rains. In one of the myths, Turquoise Woman makes the sun with turquoise beads from her right breast and the moon with white shells from her left breast.

Another version of the Navajo origin myth tells of First Man and his magic corn bundle which held four jewels, white shell, turquoise, coral or abalone, and jet, shaped like perfect ears of corn. From the magic medicine bundle came the inner forms of the earth, Long-Life Boy and Happiness Girl, who gave birth to Changing Woman, the Turquoise Goddess.

From the bundle came the forms and spirits of all things. First Man also produced the jewel poles of the hogan, the circular Navajo house built of poles and earth. (Turquoise was found beneath supporting timbers in ancient Pueblo ruins; today, pieces of turquoise or shell are placed beneath the door posts of new hogans.)

They (the Zunis) perform rites and sacrifices to certain idols; but what they most worship is water, to which they offer painted sticks and plumes, or bunches of wild flowers; and this they do commonly at springs. They also offer turquoises, which are, however, poor in quality. From the writings of Castaneda who was with Coronado in 1540

From myth to ceremony to protective charm, turquoise has exerted its magic power: as part of the medicine man's bundle and as a remedy in healing the sick; as adornment on a planting stick to assure a good crop; as a charm on the bow of a baby's cradle board to ward off evil. Fetishes of turquoise or of stone trimmed with turquoise were carried by sheepherders to make sure that flocks increased and were kept from harm. It is said that of one who wears turquoise: the lightning will not strike him, the rattlesnake will not bite him.

Turquoise was of important symbolic use to the Indians in assuring their harmonious relationship with nature, with their fellow-creatures of mother earth. Before the medicine man gathered seeds or leaves or roots, he gained assent from the plants and the earth from which they came, offering ceremonial prayers and songs and gifts of pollen, turquoise and shell. A tree, before being cut, was asked permission and was given a special drink to ease the pain of the axe. With the tree, as with the deer which has been killed, turquoise was presented to the spirit to help in regeneration.

There are spirits in all the things of the world, in all forms of life, and the Indians sought to live in harmony with nature and the great powers of the earth—to walk the way of beauty. There is the beauty of the land and all the things in it and above it and around it. There is the beauty within and the beauty without, the inner spirit and the outer form. Beauty is a way of life. And beauty is also happiness, health, harmony and peace. Turquoise is a symbol of this beauty and is part of the matrix of creation.

It has been told that as the Ant People were preparing to take their bundles of dry earth and grass seeds to the upper world, First Woman told them to take bits of the hard, blue stone of the sky so there would also be some hard rock in the new world. So when the Ant People went through the sky tunnel, they bit off pieces of the blue rock and carried them to the surface of the muddy island. And so it is that we can still find beautiful blue turquoise. From a Zuni myth

Turquoise is part of the earth, and like the Indians of the American Southwest, shaped by the forces of heat and water and stress that have formed the land.

Magmas, the molten mixtures of minerals welling up from deep below the surface, produced the crust of the earth, the igneous rocks in which turquoise is found, and the primary minerals which helped to form it.

The many kinds of rocks which contain turquoise, such as granites, porphyry, feldspars, limestone and shale, are found throughout the world. However, turquoise is formed only under special conditions; it is a mineral of desert regions and arid climates, occurring often at considerable elevations. It also often appears in connection with copper deposits. When the forces of nature created the great American Southwest, they created a special land where turquoise could form.

Most turquoise is found within the first hundred feet of the surface of the ground, occurring as veins, seams, nodules and nuggets in crevices and fissures and along fractures and faults of deeply altered rocks, usually in association with limonite, kaolinite or forms of quartz. It is a secondary mineral, resulting from nature's alterations of previously existing minerals. Turquoise is formed by the action of surface water filtering down through the earth, bringing together aluminum and phosphorus, copper and sometimes iron.

In technical terms, turquoise is a hydrous basic copper aluminum phosphate, often containing iron. The phosphorous comes from apatite, a phosphate of calcium which occurs in veins with quartz, feldspar and iron ores. Feldspar, an aluminum silicate, is the source of the alumina. Chalcopyrite, a brassy almost golden mineral and common copper ore, provides the copper.

The blue of turquoise comes from the copper and the presence of iron results in green colorations and, in some cases in a deepening of the blue. Turquoise blue has achieved its own identity as a unique color, though it is often compared to sky blue or robin's egg blue. And in literature, there is the recurring reference to heavenly blue. Turquoise varies in color from almost white, pale blue and pale blue-green to deep blue, dark green and almost purple.

Turquoise is a comparatively soft stone, yet is resistant enough to scratching to qualify as a gem. In hardness, it is rated about six on Mohs' scale. It is opaque and has a porcelain-like luster which tends to be waxy. In general, bright

St. George the Dragonslayer was often shown in paintings and tapestries with a turquoise in the hilt of his mighty sword.

Shakespeare wrote of "the compassionate turquoise that doth tell, By looking pale, its wearer is not well." Shylock had a magical turquoise ring which he said he would not have given "for a wilderness of monkeys." However, its great powers did not give him warning that his daughter would run away with his money.

During the early 19th century, wealthy young Frenchmen would occasionally wear turquoise earrings to prevent eye diseases.

A French scientist, Buffon, wrote in 1802, of the custom of wearing turquoise for good fortune and prosperity, "while not harmful, is only a sign of stupidity."

During the Victorian period, necklaces of turquoise beads were presented to newborn children as a gift of good luck.

Tagore, the Hindu poet and philosopher, wrote that to ensure enormous wealth, one should look long at the new moon, then instantly fix one's eyes on a turquoise.

In Aztec legend the god Quetzalcoatl was born after his mother swallowed a turquoise. It was he who taught the Aztecs to cut and polish *chalchihuitl,* the name for jade (nephrite) and/or turquoise. *Teoxihuitl* is the Aztec word for turquoise of the gods, when used as burial adornment. *Quetzal chalchihuitl* is used to specify blue turquoise. Aztec stone tools and pottery fragments have been found at the Cerrillos mine, Mt. Chalchihuitl, in what is now New Mexico.

Though *turquoise* is a French word, the Venetians are said to have been the first to give name to the 'stone from Turkey' or Turkestan, which included Persia, the source of the turquoise known to Europe. The glassmakers of Venice were among the most skilled at producing imitations of the blue-green gem.

blue stones are considered to be the hardest, and the color to be the most stable.

Turquoise of a single, clear color and free of associated matter is relatively rare. Most stones carry material of the matrix or mother rock in which they are found. *Turquoise matrix* is the name given to stones in which the turquoise and associated materials are intermingled and cannot be separated. Often, limonite, a yellow-brown iron-bearing mineral, and hematite, a reddish iron ore, flow through the turquoise in dense, fine-lined networks. Gems carrying these dark, geometric patterns are called *spider web turquoise.* Bits of quartz and iron pyrite are on occasion found in the stones, adding a sparkle and sometimes, golden highlights to the polished turquoise.

Turquoise is subject to many atmospheric and physical hazards. The gem can weather on exposure to sun and air, and paler stones, especially, may lose color and crumble. Water temporarily intensifies the color and Indians were said to search the ground for turquoise after a rain shower. Contact with oils, perspiration, handcreams, lotions and water with soap or detergent can alter the color. Oils penetrating the lighter, more porous parts of a stone can also make the color more even and uniform through the turquoise. During the latter half of the 19th century Pueblo Indians were known to have soaked turquoise in tallow or grease to improve the color.

With the increasing use and demand for turquoise after the beginning of this century, many methods of treating turquoise were developed. It was discovered that iodine brushed on a stone would stain the matrix and would not wash out. This method was sometimes used to enhance and deepen the rich brown color of limonite veins in turquoise. Turquoise of lesser quality was shipped to Germany, where specialists would dye and treat the stones and often shape and polish them, before sending them back to the Southwest for use in Indian-made jewelry.

Several methods of treating and stabilizing turquoise have been used, including: immersing in melted paraffin for one or two hours, which imparts greenish tints to the softer matrix and gives the stones the appearance of having been worn for some time; bonding with colloidal silica, which leaves the stones with a paler, more natural color; and bonding under pressure with alkyd resin. Modern methods do not add color or dye, but through deep, chemical vapor penetration bring up the color from within the stone itself.

Today, it is estimated that only about twenty-five per cent of mined turquoise can be used without prior treatment. Approximately ten per cent can be classed as superior gem quality and about fifteen per cent as good. Some seventy-five per cent is treated or stabilized to improve color and density. The treated stones become more durable, and the color is somewhat more permanent.

...and mines of turquoise that the Indians work, since for them they are diamonds and precious stones. Father Geronimo de Zarate Salmeron, missionary in New Mexico 1618-1626.

How and when the Indians first discovered turquoise, or began mining, are hidden in the mists of time. Over 200 ancient mines of the Indians have been rediscovered. There seem to be, in fact, few sources of turquoise in the American Southwest which were not previously mined by the Indians. The quality of craftsmanship in artifacts found in prehistoric ruins suggests that the Indians had been working with turquoise since the early centuries of this era.

Turquoise was of such importance to the Indians that those from areas without turquoise would walk long distances to regions which had mines, just as they would make their legendary journeys in search of salt. The people of Mesa Verde in southern Colorado and of Pueblo Bonito in northwest New Mexico were said to have made long pilgrimages for gems.

Since prehistoric times, trade both in turquoise and shell covered great distances. Shell was brought from the Gulf of Mexico and the Gulf of California to the Indians in Arizona, New Mexico and southern Utah and Colorado. A Franciscan father during the 18th century wrote of meeting a Hopi Indian on his way to the west coast of California to trade turquoise for abalone shell.

Turquoise unearthed at Pueblo Bonito is said to have come from mines south of Santa Fe, in the Cerrillos area, an area which is just beyond the present borders of the Santo Domingo Pueblo grant. A Navajo legend tells of a spring near Cerrillos, Yoh-toh or Bead Spring, where the first earth-born turquoise was found. The first turquoise of all was brought up from the underworld. As late as the nineteenth century, Navajos taking blankets to the Santo Domingos to trade for turquoise would stop by the spring and offer prayers "to the water, to the earth it springs from, and to the great spirits of earth and sky."

The most notable and extensive mine in this area was on Mt. Chalchihuitl. The Keres name for the mountain was *Cuwimi Kai,* 'a house inside which turquoise is found.' The Pueblo Indians and the Navajos referred to it as the place where turquoise is dug.

Thousands of tons of rock were dug out of the mountain in search of gems; one estimate is over one hundred thousand tons. Stone hammers and sledges were the mining tools and reed baskets and hide buckets were used to carry the heavy rock out of the mine, which had tunnels as deep as 400 feet.

During the 17th century the Spanish used Indian slaves to work the mine for turquoise and other minerals. One of the immediate causes of the Pueblo Revolt against the Spanish in 1680 is said to have been a collapse within the mine which resulted in the death of several of the Indians.

For a long period after the rebellion, this, and all mines, seem to have been closed. During the 18th century, the Spanish began working some mines, but within a few years were forced out of the Southwest and Mexico. For over a hundred years the mines were abandoned, so that in the latter years of the 19th century, the prehistoric mines could be "rediscovered" by American prospectors and geologists. The Indians

The ancient Egyptians also had a blue enamel which they called 'false turquoise' and which was used in faience.

Although turquoise has its own character and is usually readily identified, there are some minerals which have sometimes been mistaken for it.

Odontolite or 'bone turquoise' is fossil ivory or bone which has become stained blue by an iron phosphate. Seldom found now, during the Middle Ages in Europe it was often confused with true turquoise.

Chrysocolla, which is also found in copper mines, varies in color from green to blue. Softer than turquoise, its hardness ranges from 2 to 4. It is usually workable as a gem only when sufficient quartz has become intermixed with it during formation.

Azurite, dark blue in color, and malachite, of varying shades of green, are usually found together in upper levels of copper mines. Azurite often forms crystals. Both are cut for ornamental use, separately or when intermixed, but rarely resemble turquoise.

Chalcedony is a general term for a smooth form of quartz, which is harder, more translucent and more glasslike in appearance than turquoise. Agate is chalcedony and at times has been artificially stained various shades of blue. Chrysoprase is a chalcedony to which nickel iron gives an apple green color, and to which copper gives blues that are sometimes similar to those of turquoise.

Lapis lazuli and lazurite are stones of such a deep blue and density that it would be rare to mistake them for turquoise.

Black turquoise or 'hliakwin' is the Zuni name for jet, which is a tough form of lignite or cannel coal. It is found in several parts of the Southwest and is sometimes imported from England. It has long been used by the Indians in jewelry and ornaments.

In 1822, an Austrian scientist, Friedrich Mohs, arranged a scale of hardness in which he assigned the value of 10 to the diamond as the hardest mineral. The numbers indicate rank of hardness, not degree; for example, the difference in degree of hardness between 10 and 9 is about the same as between 9 and 1. Minerals having the same number can scratch each other as well as those of a lesser number. Talc, the softest, has a rank of 1. Some gems and their numbers are: ruby and sapphire 9, topaz 8, agate 7 and moonstone 6.

had lost their mines, first to the Spanish, and then to the white Americans. For a brief moment early in this century two groups of Indians reasserted their right to turquoise from Cerrillos mines. Four Cochiti were captured by the mine owners and sent to prison. In 1910 a group of Santo Domingo Indians took turquoise from one of the mines on Mt. Chalchihuitl but were not apprehended.

Turquoise deposits are generally not extensive, seams and veins tend to be thin, and as the Indians knew, great quantities of overburden must be removed in order to reach the gem material. In addition to the uncertainties of quantities and qualities of turquoise deposits and the hard work of reaching the gem material, there are the hardships found in the arid, desert regions where turquoise is found. The individual miners, smaller operators and even rockhounds, who contribute to the supply of turquoise are often restricted by location and weather to working only certain times during the year.

Much of the turquoise in the Southwest today is uncovered by the heavy equipment that rips up the earth in open-pit copper mines in Arizona, New Mexico and Colorado.

Although modern machinery and mining techniques can produce more turquoise than could the stone hammers and primitive methods of the prehistoric Indians, supplies continue to vary from year to year.

During recent years, demand for turquoise and particularly turquoise jewelry created by the Indians of the American Southwest has been increasing in this country and in many areas of the world. This demand has not only increased the prices and supplies of American turquoise, but also the amount of turquoise imported from Persia.

. . . and there were brought before the spirits, garments embroidered in many colors, rare necklaces of sacred shells with many turquoises and coral-like stones, all that would have made glorious the most beautifully clad of our ancients.
Zuni folk tale, Foster Child of the Deer

Turquoise jewelry and ornaments, with white and red shell and black and red stone, weave a colorful pattern that can be traced in the cultures of the ancient peoples of the American Southwest and in the myths and legends of the Indians who dwell in the land today.

Turquoise treasures have been discovered in desert sands, in burial pits and prehistoric ruins throughout Arizona, and New Mexico and in southern Colorado, Nevada and Utah. At Pueblo Bonito in Chaco Canyon in northwest New Mexico, room after room contained turquoise, unworked and in various stages of being ground and polished and as finished beads and pendants. There were also lapidary tools, shaft drills for boring holes and stones for grinding and polishing. One discovery was a fourteen-inch, four-strand necklace of 2,500 turquoise beads together with matched ear pendants.

At Ridge Ruin, near Flagstaff, Arizona, one of the finds was a small cylindrical basket covered with more than fifteen hundred bits of turquoise as a background for a design made of porcupine incisor teeth. Wooden combs with mosaics of turquoise, jet and shell were found at Hawikuh, one of the ancestral homes of the Zuni.

A Hohokam pot, unearthed in central Arizona, contained more than twelve hundred turquoise beads, several pendants and a quantity of shell and bird figure ornaments. Shell bracelets with turquoise mosaics and pendants and ear ornaments of overlays or mosaics on wood, stone and seashell have been found in ruins throughout the region. Prehistoric fetishes carved in the form of birds, frogs, toads, snakes and animals suggest the work of the modern-day descendants of the ancient craftsmen.

From the ancient beginnings until recent historical times, the Indians of the American Southwest made jewelry without the use of metal. Nuggets, chunks or nodules of turquoise were sometimes used in their natural shape with only little smoothing of the rough edges; pieces of turquoise taken from seams or veins would be shaped and smoothed, and some used for carvings. A hole worked through a stone and a length of fiber cord or leather would make the piece ready for use as a necklace, wristlet or ear pendant.

Cylindrical beads and discoidal (flat, circular, disc-like) beads would first be shaped by chipping with rock or horn before being drilled. The pieces of bead broken at this stage would have been put aside for some ceremonial use or for mosaic. In the beginning, holes were probably drilled by working a point of quartz or jasper against the softer turquoise. The first drills were probably simple sticks or shafts of wood, with one end split to hold a sharp bit of rock. Holes would be made by twirling the drill with the fingers, cutting first one side and then the other of the stone or shell. The pump or reciprocating drill was a later development.

After the beads were shaped and drilled, they would be strung tightly on a cord or thong. The entire string of beads was then rolled back and forth on a moistened slab of sandstone to make the beads smooth and uniform. Fine sand was also used for fine polishing, and sometimes ground hematite, much as jewelers' rouge is used today.

Mosaics or overlays were made on pieces of wood, stone or seashell. Bits of turquoise, jet or lignite, red and white shell, red shale, even bits of pottery were glued to the various surfaces with pinyon gum or pitch to create the designs.

While in search of the Seven Cities of Cibola in what is now New Mexico, Fray Marcos de Niza wrote in 1539 "of the number of turquoises worn as ornaments by the people. Some had as many as three or four strings of green stones around their neck; others carried them as ear-pendants and in their noses." The journal of Coronado in 1540 noted the turquoises of good quality and "turquoise earrings, combs and tablets set with turquoises."

Jewelry-making among the Indians continued in the ancient ways during the domination of the Spanish conquerors. The *conquistadores* brought horses, sheep and metals, but not the skills of the European jewelers and goldsmiths. The Indians learned something of the use of metals and metalworking

Over 5,000 years ago, ancient Egyptians were mining turquoise in the Sinai Peninsula, the desert wilderness through which the children of Israel were later to make their exodus from the land of the Pharaohs. Mines were located high on the red sandstone walls of the dry river canyon of Wadi Magharah, on the elevated plateau of Sarabit el Khadim, and in the region near the Wells of Moses between Suez and Mount Sinai. The mines were first worked with flint tools and in time, with copper chisels and stone hammers. Copper and malachite were also mined in this area once known as the Land of Turquoise. The little turquoise now found here is usually of poor quality.

The first Persian turquoise is said to have been found during ancient times in the mountains of Nishapur in a volcanic cave named after Shadad, a powerful ruler of the period. There are countless mines in the mountain range and according to ancient tradition, Isaac, the miraculous son of Abraham, was the first to open one of the mines. Nishapur is famous also as the birthplace of Omar Khayam. Much of the turquoise is found enclosed in limonite or yellow ochre, or in a whitish crust of weathered material which must be removed in order to judge the stones. In some newly-opened mines turquoise is found which pales almost to white in a short time after being exposed to air. The characteristic color of Persian turquoise is robin's egg blue and the stones are generally of fine quality. The Persian (Iranian) mines, usually located between 4,000 and 6,000 feet above sea level, are still active today and during recent years, increasing quantities of turquoise have been sent to the United States.

Pliny wrote in 77 A.D. of *callaina* (turquoise), "the most favorite ornament of the Carmanians (people of Kerman in Persia)", "which grew upon its native rock in shape like an eye, was cut, not ground into shape, set off gold better than any other gem, was spoilt by wetting with oil, grease or wine, and was the easiest of all to imitate in glass."

Marco Polo told of a province near Tibet, where there was a mountain "whence are quarried turquoise stones in great abundance, very large and beautiful."

Four bracelets of gold and turquoise created by Egyptian goldsmiths more than 5,000 years ago were found in the tomb of King Zer at Abydos. Two of the bracelets carry round and cylindrical beads of turquoise and amethyst. One includes lapis lazuli with the turquoise. The fourth has small falcon figures rising from alternate blocks of gold and turquoise. The falcon was the symbol of the early sun-god Horus.

The interior of a jeweler's workroom is shown in a wall painting in an ancient tomb near the pyramids of Gizeh. The master weighs gemstones on scales, workers kneel before a clay furnace and use long blow pipes to keep the fire glowing, others beat gold into sheets, while some form and solder the gold into jewelry, and one grinds and polishes bits of sky-blue turquoise for inlay work.

The diadem of an Egyptian princess of the twelfth dynasty was formed like a garland of flowers with five roses of cloisonne' gold inlaid with red carnelian and turquoise and a hundred fifty flowerets in gold, carnelian and turquoise.

The innermost case of the sarcophagus of King Tutankhamen and the mask of the mummy were of solid beaten gold inlaid with carnelian, lapis lazuli and turquoise. His throne was fashioned of wood, with overlays of gold and inlays of blue and green glass, carnelian, lapis lazuli and turquoise. Turquoise was used also in rings found in the tomb, in a diadem and in a large pectoral or breast ornament.

tools from the Spanish, and during the first half of the nineteenth century, they began to make some ornaments and bracelets from copper and brass. Copper and brass pots that came into the region from Mexico and lengths of copper wire obtained from traders were pounded into the flat sheets from which the bracelets and pendants were formed. The ornamental pieces would occasionally be decorated with a piece of stone or shell or with designs filed or scratched into the metal.

Working with silver by the Indians first began in the latter half of the nineteenth century. According to the Franciscan Fathers in their *Ethnologic Dictionary of the Navajo Language,* published in 1910, "a Navaho blacksmith, known by his own people as Atsidi Sani, or 'the old smith', and by the Mexicans as Herrero, or 'the smith', first learned the art from a Mexican silversmith named Cassilo."

It is believed that Atsidi Sani first learned to work with iron in 1853 at the American army base, Fort Defiance in Arizona near the border of New Mexico. He is known to have been one of the Navajos rounded up by Kit Carson in 1863, and imprisoned at Fort Sumner at Bosque Redondo, New Mexico, until the establishment of the Navajo reservation in 1868. Just when he learned to work with silver is not known for certain, but shortly after his release, he set up shop as a silversmith.

Atsidi Sani was said to have been interested primarily in producing the silver bridle ornaments which the Navajos regularly bought from Mexican silversmiths. He is said to have taught the craft to his four sons, as well as several fellow Navajos. One of his pupils was Atsidi Chon, a Navajo who moved to Zuni in 1872. While at Zuni, he taught silver work to Lanyade, a Zuni ironworker, and Lanyade, in turn, taught Sikyatala, a Hopi.

Thus, the Indians of the American Southwest made silversmithing a part of their culture. They worked with the tools and equipment they could adapt from materials at hand, or that they could get their hands on. The first stone anvils were replaced by pieces of iron or railroad track; an old shovel could serve as a crucible for melting silver, and the silver might come from the silverware of a railroad restaurant, Mexican pesos or American dollars. The Navajos preferred the purer silver of the pesos; the dollar contained more copper which gave a yellowish cast to the silver. And during the 1890's, the U.S. government began to enforce a law banning the use of silver money for jewelry.

Atsidi Chon is said to have made the first silver belt, and he is attributed with the first use of turquoise with silver in 1878, when he attached a turquoise to a silver ring.

For the next several years, the Indian craftsmen produced ornaments and jewelry primarily for themselves or for trade to other Indians. Production was limited, in part, because they were working with primitive tools and were still mastering the new craft, but more, because they had little money with which to buy silver and had little turquoise available.

The Indians had not been in control of the turquoise mines since the days of the Spanish conquistadores. After the collapse of the Cerrillos mine and the 1680 rebellion against the

Spanish, all mines seem to have been closed. The country was under U.S. domination when the mines were being rediscovered in the latter part of the nineteenth century, and ownership remained in private, non-Indian hands.

The Indian silversmiths made use of turquoise from old ornamental pieces and the few new stones were shaped and polished in the traditional way. In the beginning both Navajo and Zuni jewelry tended to be massive; the silver heavy and simple, the single large stone held in a high bezel (the narrow silver strips which hold the setting to the ring, bracelet or ornament).

The Navajos called silver "the metal of the moon." For the Navajo smiths silver was the important element in the design; the function of turquoise was to enhance the beauty of the silver. They could be content just working with silver and decorating it with designs filed into a piece or stamped in with dies they had cut. Turquoise might be used if they could afford or find a stone big enough and good enough to suit their taste.

The Navajos became skilled in the art of casting, cutting designs into two-part molds of sandstone or volcanic tuff. Molten silver would be carefully poured into the form so that it would flow into all parts of the design. After cooling, the cast silver would be removed from the molds, smoothed and polished.

Single molds carved into charred wood or sandstone were also used, often for casting bracelets.

Carved wood forms were used in making wrought, or hammered, pieces. Hollow beads were made by soldering together two hemispheres of silver which had been hammered on hardwood in which various sizes and designs had been cut.

. . . his heavy anklets of sacred white shell; his blue turquoise earrings, like the sky in blueness, and so long that they swept his shoulders . . .

Silver bead necklaces were among the first pieces of jewelry made by the Navajo craftsmen, the beads formed in many cases from Mexican pesos. Squash blossoms, the Navajos call them "beads that spread out," became distinctive elements in many necklaces. The delicate, bell-shaped flower is in some stories described as a symbol of fertility and the promise of bountiful harvest. And with the Hopi, the whorl style of the maidens' hairdress is said by some to have been inspired by the squash blossom. The bead form is sometimes attributed to the design of the decorative buttons which adorned the outer seams of Spanish officers' trousers, a design based upon the flower of the pomegranate, for which Granada, Spain is named. Whatever the origin, the accepted name for bead and necklaces is *squash blossom*.

Naja (nahja, najahe), the crescent or horseshoelike pendant often found on necklaces is said to have come from a bridle ornament which was brought to Mexico by the Spanish. It was a device meaning "Godspeed" or good-luck which came to Spain with the Moors, who considered it a holy symbol representing the hands of Fatima, the daughter of Mohammed. Just as the silversmiths have created a variety of squash blos-

A carnelian (red chalcedony) necklace of about 1400 B.C. carries a single teardrop-shaped turquoise, miniature lizard and alligator figures and seed shapes formed from gold.

The jewelers of the Egyptian pharaohs engraved turquoise for use on bracelets and necklaces. Vases were shaped of gold and inlaid with turquoise.

Necklaces of shell and bone were made by the prehistoric ancestors of the Persians. After the discovery of metal, bracelets and necklaces were made of copper and often inset with stones.

The metalworkers of Luristan created belt plaques, bracelets and anklets of bronze decorated with animal forms, such as lions, rams, and ibex with curving horns.

Goldsmiths at a later period continued to make animal forms and would inlay gems in armlets, bracelets, collars and necklaces.

Rings, pendants, earrings and necklaces of gold were created with decorations of filigree, colored enamels, and gems. The jewelry workers also created ornaments with designs using niello. Niello is a black metallic substance made from silver, copper, lead and sulphur. The design is incised into gold or silver and filled with the black substance, creating a contrast between the darkened design and the bright metal.

Metal bottles and vases and warriors' helmets were overlaid with gold and encrusted with gems, including turquoise.

Although few examples of the jewelry remain, manuscripts, from the 14th century on, are filled with colorful illustrations showing the ornament and jewelry of the Persians.

Etruscan and Greek gold bracelets and earrings have been found, decorated with pendants in the form of lions' heads, lotus and pomegranate blossoms.

During the Hellenistic period, Roman jewelry used large colored stones in the center of designs; smaller stones were cut in simple shapes and grouped in rows by color, red, green or blue. Gold rings dating from this period have been found with cameos carved in turquoise.

soms, so have they varied their designs of the naja, while maintaining the basic crescent shape.

The *ketoh,* which is now worn as a bracelet by the Indians, was the ancient leather guard to protect the wrist from the sting of the bowstring. The Navajos were the first to decorate the broad leather bowguard with silver.

Concha, the Spanish word for shell, is a round shell-like medallion which the Navajos have long used in making belts. Mexican bridle ornaments may have provided the initial inspiration, though some experts contend that the original conchas were hair ornaments worn by the Plains Indians, who received them from the French. The first Navajo conchas had a barred center opening through which a leather belt could be threaded. The Navajo smiths subsequently did away with the center opening and by placing the bar at the back of the conchas provided the entire front surface for decoration.

Rings have long been crafted by the Navajos, and in their language there are names for eighteen different types of rings. For the most part, Navajo rings are characterized by massive silver with a single large turquoise of irregular shape.

Around the beginning of this century, more turquoise became available to the Indian silversmiths, and within a few years almost all of their work was decorated with one or more pieces of turquoise.

... she had everything a Zuni maiden could wish for—blankets and moccasins, turquoise earrings and shell necklaces, bracelets so many you could not count them.

Much of the turquoise was soft and easy to work, and in contrast to hard stones of good quality, could be cut into smaller stones without losing value. For the Zuni, this meant the opportunity once again to practice the lapidary art as had their ancestors.

In their early work the Zuni followed the pattern of the Navajo, creating heavy silver pieces with a single large stone. Now, the turquoise became increasingly more important than the silver in the work of the Zuni craftsmen. Whereas earlier the turquoise had been used to enhance the silver, now the silver was used to set off the beauty of turquoise. Zuni jewelry began to carry several small turquoises around a larger central stone, and then many small pieces arranged together or in linear patterns around rings and bracelets. Silverwork became daintier, through design and because of greater skill in the art as well as better tools. The Zuni usually did not use dies to stamp designs into their silver, but made silver wire twists, loops and borders as decoration.

By the 1920's, the Zuni craftsmen had set the direction of their style: intricate, more delicate silverwork dominated by turquoise, usually, many small stones.

Cluster, the setting of quantities of small, shaped stones in geometric patterns around a larger central stone, is a favored Zuni design form. Each stone is held in its own silver bezel in the cluster. *Needlepoint,* slender stones coming to points at each end, is a cluster form which developed during the late

30's and early 40's. *Petit point* is a later version in which the turquoise may be finished with one pointed end and one round end, or as small ovals or even as small round stones.

Channel is a Zuni technique which first appeared late in the 20's and grew in popularity from the middle 40's on. In channel work, strips of silver are soldered to a silver base to form small cells or partitioned areas, (the French call them *cloison*). Bits of turquoise or other jewelry materials are fitted into the tiny cells, and then the entire piece is polished at the same time so that the silver dividing walls and stones present a uniform, smooth surface. Usually the surface is flat, though sometimes it is given a cabochon or slightly rounded form. The silver dividers in channel jewelry show between the stones as part of the design; whereas, in mosaic, the pieces of turquoise and other materials are fitted against one another to create a design without separations.

Mosaic, a design form which dates back to prehistoric times, was revived by the Zunis in the mid-1930's and applied to modern jewelry. Turquoise, white and red shell and jet were used in mosaic pieces found in the ancient Zuni pueblo of Hawikuh; the present-day Zunis also make use of mother-of-pearl, abalone shell, coral, and on occasion, cannel coal from England and even, at one period, old phonograph records. Mosaic provides the opportunity for creating a variety of designs and shapes. Some of the designs are inspired by the ancient gods or animal spirits, but there is no religious significance attached to the jewelry. The rainbow god and the god of the zenith (the so-called Thunderbird or Knife-wing bird) have long been popular designs. Now, there are many sources for creations in mosaic, such as kachina masks, dragonflies, sun shields, birds and animals, and occasionally scenes from everyday life.

The Zunis have long been skilled at carving fetishes, creating symbolic figures to protect against harm, to cure illness and, in general, to bring good luck. Birds, turtles, frogs, bears, lizards, and mountain lions are among the figures carved. Size of figures used on necklaces is small, from one-half to one inch in length. Today, many of the figurines used in necklaces have no significance as fetishes, but are good examples of careful artisanship. Coral, jet, and other materials are now used in addition to turquoise.

Mosaic, inlay, channel, cluster work of all kinds, find application in most types of jewelry and ornament: necklaces, earrings, pendants, bracelets, rings, pins, buckles, concha belts, and since the 1950's on bola ties.

The Santa Domingos are known for their craft of making fine beads, which are called *hishi* (heishe, heshi). Olivella, clam and abalone shell are used, and just as in ancient times, small bits of shell are drilled, strung together and rolled over a piece of sandstone to smooth and round the edges. Turquoise beads or discs are also produced in much the same manner, though the two faces of the turquoise are also polished. Turquoise is sometimes included with the shell in necklaces, which may have pendants composed of several strands of *jocla* (jacloh). Jocla is the name for ear loops, which, when not worn on the ear, are hung from the necklaces as added deco-

In medieval Europe, rings were fashioned of metal and decorated with stones to represent the planets: Jupiter was tin with carnelian, Venus was copper with amethyst and Saturn was lead with turquoise.

During the 15th century the Queen of France gave a gold ring set with turquoise to King James IV of Scotland as a pledge of friendship and regard, and for his help with Henry the Eighth. The belief that turquoise protects the wearer from falls and wounds did not hold true for James. He was wearing the turquoise ring when he was killed at the battle of Flodden Field in August 1513.

During the time of the Medicis, turquoise cameos appeared on brooches and pendants. The portraits of Greek goddesses were carved on the matrix, the blue of the turquoise serving as background.

The Taj Mahal, which took thirteen years to build, from 1632 to 1645, is adorned with gems from many parts of the world, among them agates from Yemen, onyx from Persia, lapis lazuli from Ceylon, coral from Arabia and turquoise from Tibet.

The ornate crown of the Tibetan queens of Sikkim is designed of intricate gold bands set with pearls, coral and turquoise. In a 1908 painting of the Maharini of Sikkim she is shown wearing the crown, gold earrings inlaid with turquoise in concentric rings, a necklace with a charmbox pendant set with rubies, lapis lazuli and turquoise, and two gold rings, one set with coral, the other with turquoise.

An advertisement in an issue of *London Gazette* in 1679 stated: 'Lost . . . a Ring with a large Turquoies of the Old Rock, very good colour.'

Samuel Pepys notes in his diary entry for February 18, 1668 that he had been shown "a ring of a Turkey-stone, set with little sparks of diamonds."

Shortly after the revolution in France, semi-precious stones seemed more appropriate for use in jewelry. Among the more popular pieces were bracelets of turquoise set around with small brilliants and joined by fine gold links.

When Sarah Bernhardt appeared as Cleopatra in a stage production in 1890, she wore several turquoise ornaments. So great was her popularity that there followed a revival of jewelry with Egyptian motifs using turquoise and oxidized silver.

During the early years of this century, jewelry sets combining Italian coral and Persian turquoise were popular in Europe and the United States.

When Queen Elizabeth II of England was married, her gift from President Aleman of Mexico was an exact replica of a prehistoric Nahuatl (Aztec) brooch of gold inlaid with turquoise.

ration.

The Hopi name for silver is *shiba* (siva), "a little white, round cake," derived perhaps from their description of the coins from which they obtained their first silver. Traditionally, the Hopis used little turquoise in their jewelry.

During the late 1930's the Hopi silversmiths developed a distinctive style called *overlay*. The method uses two pieces of silver: the top or overlay has a cutout design, the area on the lower piece directly below the design is oxidized or blackened, creating a contrast between the bright and the dark silver. Designs were drawn in many cases from pottery decoration.

Today, the tribal differences in design and use of materials are useful, primarily, for giving names to styles or techniques. A piece may be described as "like Zuni" or "like Navajo," although in practice it may have been made by a craftsman or craftswoman of another tribe, or may have combined the jewel work of a Zuni with the silver work of a Navajo. Turquoise jewelry and ornament are now created by Zuni, Hopi, Santo Domingo, Santa Clara, San Juan and other Pueblo Indian craftsmen and craftswomen, as well as the Navajo.

They are inspired by ancestral motifs and designs, but they are not bound by tradition. The new craft of silversmithing provided a release from the old ways of making jewelry and ornaments, as well as a freedom to create new forms.

The use of turquoise with silver added a new, or rather, an old element in a new context. The reverence for turquoise became a love for the decorative beauty of the stone. The ceremonial meaning of the stone was not forgotten, but in jewelry, turquoise became an element of design.

As craftsmen, the Indians share a common knowledge of tools and techniques and as artists, they learn and are inspired by one another. They gain knowledge from study in schools and colleges and travels to other areas, and they gain inspiration from their own developing skills and creative insights. Today, the craftsman is no longer an Indian who happens to be an artist, but rather, an artist who happens to be Indian.

In happiness and beauty may fair corn of all colors come with you to the ends of the earth/In happiness and beauty may fair plants of all kinds come with you to the ends of the earth/ In happiness and beauty may fair jewels of all kinds come with you to the ends of the earth.

Hopi village of Walpi, built shortly after 1680, on First Mesa in Arizona.

Helen Long, Navajo weaver,
silversmith and matriarch of a
family of silversmiths.

Pueblo and Navajo necklaces showing early silver work, stylings of
squash blossoms and the use of red trade beads. Cross necklace, on left,
from Isleta Pueblo, was collected by a Franciscan priest in 1868.

Prehistoric stone and turquoise beads and turquoise bird carving date from 1100 to 1250 A.D. Necklace of turquoise on yucca leaf twine was made prior to 900 A.D.

Turquoise mosaic in prehistoric jewelry made by the Salado and Anasazi between 1100 and 1400 A.D.: glycymeris sea shell bracelets; bone hair pieces; and seashell pendants. Walnut Black-on-white Anasazi pottery cup was made between 1100 and 1250 A.D.

Pueblo jewelry handcrafted between 1860 and 1880. Materials are shell, jet, wood, copper and turquoise. Santo Domingo necklace in left foreground carries Cerrillos turquoise.

Zuni and Navajo bracelets and necklaces of the 1940's and 50's, with examples of Zuni channel work, including the use of coral with turquoise. Bracelet with horseshoe design reflects commercial and tourist influence on Indian jewelry.

Classic example of Zuni jewelry of the 1920's.

Zuni mosaic inlay of the late 1930's. Seashells formed the foundation
for the turquoise, jet and shell inlay and then, in many cases, were set in
heavy silver. Concha belt was made by Lambert Homer.

Navajo jewelry from 1860's through 1890's. Brass and copper bracelets show early use of metal. Ketoh, from about 1875, is an example of silver worked with crude hand-made tools. Pieces with turquoise were fashioned during the 1880's and 90's. Jar is Hopi pottery from the late 1800's.

Strands of hishi, wampum, coral, turquoise, stone and shell, handcrafted between 1860 and 1940, show the patina from wear and handling. Typical of "old pawn" jewelry found in pawn vaults during the early 1900's.

Navajo and Pueblo jewelry of early 1900's to late 1920's fashioned from coin silver and with stones that had been hand cut, drilled and polished. Coral, already cut and polished came from Italy. Hopi jar, made by Nampeyo, is from about 1905.

Classic squash blossom necklaces of late 1880's to early 1900's. In background: old Navajo wedding basket and Navajo woman's dress.

Jewelry from about 1885 to early 1900's. Multiple stones in bracelets first began to appear around the turn of the century. Turquoise stones shown here are all hand cut and polished; most are probably green and blue Cerrillos turquoise.

Navajo and Zuni jewelry of the late 1920's and 30's, showing the abundant
use of turquoise and examples of the popular cluster style.

Hopi Butterfly dancer
Wilmer Saufkie.

Navajo hogan in Monument Valley, Arizona. Silhouetted rocks are the
Three Sisters.

Morenci open pit copper mine near Arizona-New Mexico border in east-central Arizona, source of Morenci turquoise.

Pawn vault at Pinon Mercantile Trading Company on the Navajo
reservation.

Coal Canyon in the Hopi-Navajo country of Arizona.

Hopi artist, Charles Loloma, noted contemporary jewelry designer, prepares a gold bezel for a gold and turquoise bracelet.

Necklace fashioned of 14-karat yellow gold with silver beads is set with green Royston turquoise.

Ore containing veins of Battle Mountain turquoise. Necklace and bracelet with high grade Battle Mountain settings, crafted by Francis James, a Navajo.

Ring and bracelet in foreground are set with Lone Mountain turquoise; top left, Number Eight spider web turquoise; top right, Lander Blue.

Bracelets set with Number Eight spider web turquoise. Cluster bracelet at lower right contains matched top grade stones.

Jewelry set with high grade Castle Dome turquoise. This unusual example of channel work was designed and crafted by Zuni artist Sherman Yuselu.

Silver work set with high grade Kingman turquoise nuggets, crafted by
Navajo artist, Jimmy Bedoni.

Navajo silver work with high grade Lander Blue turquoise.

Three bracelets of high grade Bisbee turquoise. Choker is made of unusual hand-cut tur- quoise beads.

Rare three-strand necklace of "fossil" turquoise. Mosaic pin created by Navajo artist Lee Yazzie has background of exceptional quality Blue Gem turquoise.

Squash blossom necklace set with Blue Gem turquoise. Large polished
stone is also Blue Gem turquoise.

Green turquoise from the old Los Cerrillos mines south of Santa Fe. Bracelet, fashioned by contemporary Hopi artist Charles Loloma, of a Cerrillos jocla with coral set in yellow gold.

Cynthia Manuel, a Pima-Papago Indian. Squash blossom necklace is set with Fox turquoise. Basket is Pima.

Left Mitten in Monument Valley, along the Arizona-Utah border.

Hishi necklaces of turquoise, gold, coral, jet, mother of pearl and shell by Charles Lovato of Santo Domingo, New Mexico. Pottery jar made by the famous Maria Martinez and her son, Popovi Da.

Fetish necklace in foreground is a classic carved by Leekya (Old Man Leekya). Bear fetish in background contains over 10,000 carats of turquoise. Old Zuni jar shows traditional designs.

Butterflies created in the inlay styling of Zuni artists Virgil and Shirley
Benn.

Necklaces with turquoise fetishes carved by David Tsikewa.

Zuni inlay using turquoise, jet, coral, mother of pearl, tortoise and abalone shell.

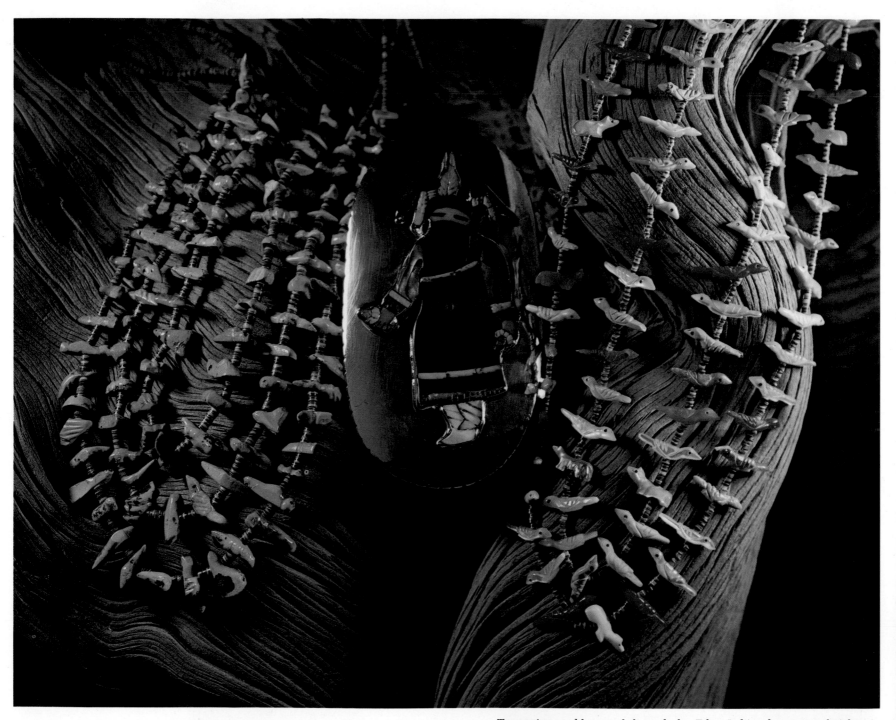

Turquoise necklace at left made by Edna Leki, who carves fetishes in the "old way", wherein stones which resemble an animal or bird are carved or embellished only slightly, to accent the already present features. Mary Tsikewa, Edna's sister, carved the fetish necklace at the right, in the "modern way", in which an animal or bird form is conceived and carved from a piece of shell or stone which previously lacked any particular life-like form. Silver box was made by Joe Chee and the inlaid Kachina Mana figure by Veronica Nastacio.

Needlepoint bracelet, left foreground, fashioned by Zuni artist Lucille Quam and four needlepoint and petit point pieces created by Navajo artists Billy and Betty Betoney, feature Kingman turquoise.

Belt buckle and bola tie set,
with inlaid designs of Apache
Gahn Dancers, created by
Zuni artist, Lon Jose.

Clusters of turquoise in jewelry crafted by Navajo and Zuni artists.

Hishi of turquoise, shell and ivory by Paul Rosetta of Santo Domingo,
New Mexico.

In Navajo country, Church Rock with rocky crags in distance.

Edward Curley, a Navajo who lives near Kaibito Trading Post in northern Arizona.

Silver and turquoise styling by Navajo artist, Eddie Begay. These are
part of an eleven-piece set.

Zuni necklace crafted by Kirk and Mary. Prehistoric Gila polychrome jar is from the ancient Salado culture.

Inlay work of Zuni master, Dennis Edaakie. Pendant in center foreground
features a red cardinal on reverse side.

Bracelets by Charles Loloma using his "ear of corn" style of stone setting; two bracelets in foreground were made in the 1960's. Initials inscribed in bracelets are marks of the owner. Turquoise hishi in background was made by Charles Lovato of Santo Domingo.

Squash blossom necklace of silver with Lone Mountain turquoise and bola tie of gold with Villa Grove turquoise created by Navajo jewelsmith Lee Yazzie. Wide Ruins Navajo rug in background.

Necklaces created by Zuni artists Lee and Mary Weebothee.

Cluster bracelet of Kingman turquoise set in yellow gold by Alice Quam of Zuni Pueblo.

Ancient pottery designs in silver overlay jewelry set with Nevada turquoise by master Hopi silversmith, Lawrence Saufkie, whose father, Paul Saufkie, Sr., was one of the first to create the Hopi overlay style. Bola tie is set with Royston turquoise.

Bracelet, set with about 700 carats of high grade Kingman turquoise, and necklace, with 14-karat gold bars and a variety of natural spider web turquoise, were fashioned by Charles Loloma.

Robin's egg blue Persian turquoise and diamonds in a gold necklace by Andrew of Scottsdale. This is an example of contemporary styling by a non-Indian artist.

Hopi overlay silver work accented with turquoise by Victor Coochwytewa
of Second Mesa, Arizona.

Sandcast concha belt and buckle by Harold Lovato of Santo Domingo set with turquoise and coral. Artifacts are from ancient Hohokam culture of central Arizona.

Navajo squash blossom necklace by Leroy Hill.

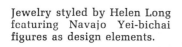

Bracelets by Santo Domingo artist, Sedelio F. Lovato: the two with inlay work are set with Morenci turquoise; the bracelet in upper left with Persian turquoise. Hishi by Charles Lovato of Santo Domingo.

Jewelry set with high grade Morenci turquoise, created by artist Larry Golsh, a Pala-Mission Indian.

Silver work set with high grade Bisbee turquoise by Navajo artist Mary Morgan.

Persian turquoise and diamonds combined with silver, yellow gold and bear claws in contemporary design by Navajo artist, Andy Kirk.

Pueblo Bonito in Chaco Canyon National Monument, New Mexico, oc-
cupied by the Anasazi between the 9th and 12th centuries A.D.

Adam Martinez, Tewa Indian,
in front of a kiva at the Pueblo
of San Ildefonso, north of
Santa Fe.

Desert big horn sheep skull covered with a variety of natural turquoise.
An old pawn necklace is in foreground.

Silver boxes with examples of Zuni inlay.

Ironwood bowl with silver and Villa Grove turquoise. Lee Weebothee did the silversmithing and Mary Webothee, the lapidary work.

Turquoise carving of Zuni war
chief, Sue be Koei, made in
1932 by Teddy Weahkee of
Zuni Pueblo.

"Blue Corn People" by Charles Pratt, Cheyenne-Arapahoe sculptor. Turquoise corn is symbolic of a plentiful harvest.

Styling and silverwork of
Preston Monongye, a Hopi-
Mission Indian, combined
with lapidary work of Sadie
Laahtie, a Zuni.

Silver jewelry boxes set with large nuggets of polished Nevada turquoise, created by Navajo craftsman John Hoxie.

Silver container set with Persian turquoise by White Buffalo, a Comanche, and a man's ring with Bisbee turquoise by Navajo craftsman, Sam Begay.

Pottery with turquoise insets created by Toni Da of San Ildefonso Pueblo, New Mexico.

Acknowledgments and Appreciations

Ashton Gallery · Scottsdale, Arizona

Andrew Designer in Gold · Scottsdale, Arizona

C. G. Wallace Collection/Heard Museum · Phoenix, Arizona

Don Hoel's · Oak Creek Canyon, Arizona

Fenn Galleries, Ltd. · Santa Fe, New Mexico

Gila River Arts & Crafts Center · Sacaton, Arizona

Goldwater's Indian Jewelry · Phoenix and
   Scottsdale, Arizona

Heard Museum Shop · Phoenix, Arizona

Hubbell Trading Post · Ganado, Arizona

Hunter's Trading Post · Phoenix, Arizona

Jonathan & Phillip Holstein

J & B Chauncey's Indian Arts · Phoenix, Arizona

Lee's Indian Crafts · Phoenix, Arizona

McGee's Indian Den · Scottsdale, Arizona

McGee Traders, Inc:
   Pinon Mercantile Trading Company · Pinon, Arizona
   Keams Canyon Arts & Crafts · Keams Canyon, Arizona

Partieh Company (Persian Turquoise Importers)
   San Francisco, Calif.

Paul Johnson Jewelers · Phoenix, Arizona

Popovi Da Studio of Indian Arts · San Ildefonso, New Mexico

Scottsdale National Indian Arts Council Exhibition
   Scottsdale, Arizona

Tanners Indian Arts · Scottsdale, Arizona and Gallup,
   New Mexico

Wampum Trading Post · Los Angeles, California

Special Appreciation

Jerold Collings

Robert Ashton

Kermit Lee

Barton Wright, curator of the Museum of Northern Arizona

Lois Jacka

*Beautiful treasures are to be found in the spirits of
those who helped in the creation of this book. Inspired by their
love of turquoise and Indian artistry, they gave unselfishly
of their time, knowledge and collections. To each of them,
I express my deepest gratitude and heartfelt thanks.*
Jerry Jacka